Marqusie

CHRISTOPHER COLUMBUS

Troll Associates

CHRISTOPHER COLUMBUS

by Rae Bains

Illustrated by Dick Smolinski

Troll Associates

Library of Congress Cataloging in Publication Data

Bains, Rae.
    Christopher Columbus.

    Summary: Explains the importance of the contribution
made by the Italian sailor and navigator Christopher
Columbus, whose discovery of America in 1492 changed the
geography of the known world.
        1. Columbus, Christopher—Juvenile literature.
2. Explorers—America—Biography—Juvenile literature.
3. Explorers—Spain—Biography—Juvenile literature.
4. America—Discovery and exploration—Spanish—Juvenile
literature. [1. Columbus, Christopher. 2. Explorers.
3. America—Discovery and exploration—Spanish]
I. Smolinski, Dick, ill.   II. Title.
E111.B15   1984   970.1'5 [B] [92]   84-2585
ISBN 0-8167-0150-4 (lib. bdg.)
ISBN 0-8167-0151-2 (pbk.)

Of all the explorers in history, none made a greater contribution to the world than Christopher Columbus. He was more than an extraordinary navigator and sailor. Columbus was a man of vision and determination.

Though he never succeeded in his original goal of finding a western route to the Far East, Columbus found a continent that no one in Europe had even dreamed about! The daring voyages that carried him to the shores of America changed the geography of the known world enormously.

Christopher Columbus was born in Genoa, Italy, in 1451. There is no record of the exact date of his birth, but it was probably between August 25 and October 31.

In Italian, his last name was *Columbo*, and his first name was *Christoforo*. Later, when he settled in Spain, Columbus was known by the name *Cristobal Colon*. But it is as Christopher Columbus that he is best known.

The first child of Domenico and Susanna Columbo, young Christopher helped his father with the family's weaving business. Columbus had little formal education, but he taught himself to read and write in Spanish and Latin. Latin was especially important in Columbus's time, because all scholarly books, maps, and charts were in Latin. In every European country, Latin was the language of learning.

Genoa, Columbus's home town, was a busy seaport. Ships going to and from places all over Europe and the rest of the world often dropped anchor in Genoa harbor. Young Christopher was fascinated by the ships and the men who sailed them. He couldn't wait to go to sea.

During Christopher's teen years, he gained experience as a sailor on a number of voyages around the Mediterranean. After each one, he returned to Genoa and his father's shop. Then, at the age of nineteen, he gave up weaving for good. He signed aboard a Genoese galley that was part of a war fleet. This gave him his first taste of military action at sea.

By the time Columbus was twenty-six years old, he had seen battle a number of times. As a sailor, he had traveled as far north as Ireland and as far into the Atlantic Ocean as Iceland. Columbus had also sailed all around the coast of Europe and part of the way down the coast of Africa. On each voyage the bright, observant seaman added to his knowledge of geography and navigation.

Columbus learned to use the crude quadrants and compasses of his time, and to read the stars and navigational charts that guided ships from port to port. He also listened carefully to the accounts of voyages taken by others. And he learned the theories about what one might find in the mysterious waters of the far Atlantic and beyond.

In Columbus's time, educated people knew very well that the Earth was not flat, and that a ship could not fall off the edge of the world. But no one had ever sailed very far into the Atlantic Ocean, which was known as the Sea of Darkness.

There were, however, some maps depicting the Earth as a globe. Christopher Columbus had seen these maps and learned much from them. He had many discussions about the sea and geography with Bartholomew, one of his younger brothers. Bartholomew ran a shop in Lisbon, Portugal, that sold navigational charts and instruments.

In the eight years between 1477 and 1485, Christopher divided his time between working in his brother's business and serving aboard various vessels. It was also during this period of time that he married Doña Felipa Perestrello e Moniz, the daughter of a wealthy Portuguese nobleman and sea captain. They had one child—a boy, whom they named Diego.

In those days, the only way to reach the Orient was by traveling overland. Gold, spices, and jewels had to be brought back to Europe the same way—and it was a long, expensive trip. Some explorers were already searching for a sea route to the Orient. They planned to reach the Orient by sailing south —down the coast of Africa—and then east across the Indian Ocean.

But Columbus came to the conclusion that it should be possible to reach the Orient by sailing west—across the Atlantic Ocean. He tried to convince the king of Portugal to finance an expedition based on his beliefs. But King John II wasn't interested.

In 1485, Columbus and five-year-old Diego moved to Spain. The boy's mother had died, and since the Portuguese government wasn't interested in Columbus's plan, there was no longer any reason to stay in Portugal. Soon after arriving in Spain, Columbus placed Diego at a boys' school run by Franciscan monks.

Columbus went on to the city of Cordova, where he hoped to obtain an audience with the Spanish queen, Isabella. It took a year before he was able to see her and her husband, King Ferdinand. When he did, Columbus presented his plan to them and explained the reasoning behind it.

Columbus told Isabella and Ferdinand that the world measured a little less than 19,000 miles around its center. Using this number, Columbus explained that the distance from Europe to Japan was no farther if one went west or east. Furthermore, he told them, making the voyage by sea would cost a great deal less than it cost to send caravans overland.

There was one major mistake in Columbus's theory, even though the king and queen didn't know it. The mistake was that the circumference of the Earth is not 19,000 miles. It is closer to 25,000 miles—a significant difference.

Moreover, Columbus thought the Earth had just one large land mass, made up of Europe and Asia, and one large ocean, the Atlantic. He had no idea of the great land mass that makes up North and South America. Nor did he suspect that there was another huge ocean, which we now call the Pacific.

In any case, Isabella and Ferdinand turned him down.

For the next six years, Columbus tried

again and again to convince Ferdinand and Isabella to finance his voyage. At last, in 1492, when Columbus was preparing to take his plan to the king of France, Isabella and Ferdinand agreed.

The Spanish royal couple gave Columbus three ships, the *Niña*, the *Pinta*, and the flagship, *Santa Maria*. They also supplied a crew of ninety seamen for the three ships and all food and provisions for the long voyage.

In addition, the agreement said that Columbus would be governor-general of all lands he discovered and claimed for Spain. Finally, Columbus could claim one tenth of all the precious stones, gold, silver, spices, and other valuable merchandise he acquired. The other nine tenths were to be turned over to the Spanish treasury.

The three ships under Columbus's command set sail from Palos, Spain, on August 3, 1492. The small fleet stopped at the Canary Islands to pick up fresh provisions, then ventured west into uncharted waters. On and on the three ships sailed.

Each day the crew grew more fearful. They were worried that the winds carrying them west might blow against them on their return and prevent them from ever sailing home. There was even a threat of mutiny. It became so serious that Columbus agreed that they would turn around if land was not sighted within three more days. This was on October 10.

Two days later, on October 12, 1492, the fleet reached the Bahama Islands, off the southeast coast of North America. Columbus named the island San Salvador and claimed it for Spain. He was sure this island was part of the Indies, off the coast of China or Japan, so he called the natives Indians. Even when his mistake was discovered, a few years later, the name continued to be used. We still call the islands off the east coast of America the West Indies. And native Americans are still called Indians.

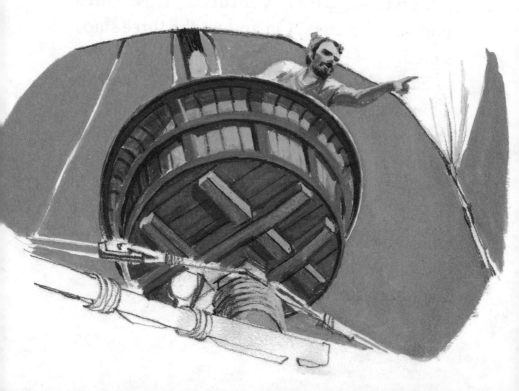

After a few days at San Salvador, the fleet sailed to Cuba and on to Hispaniola. There, Columbus established a small colony. He then set sail for Europe in January 1493. Only the *Niña* and *Pinta* were making the return voyage. The *Santa Maria* had been wrecked off the coast of Hispaniola. Two months later, after a harrowing voyage, the ships reached Spain.

Although Columbus did not bring back a treasure of gold and jewels, he did have some West Indian natives to present to the king and queen. Even more important, he had proved that land could be reached by sailing west. Isabella and Ferdinand were delighted. They ordered Columbus to organize another voyage, to explore and colonize new lands for Spain.

Columbus led three more expeditions to the New World, in 1493, 1498, and 1502. Each time, he discovered additional territories—Jamaica, Trinidad, and many locations along the coasts of Central and South America. But he never found the treasures of the Orient.

The Spaniards who had colonized the new territories had traveled to the New World only to become rich. They became angry and disillusioned. The failure to find treasure also disappointed the king and queen of Spain. And so, the titles promised to Columbus were taken away. He was in disgrace. Then, when Queen Isabella died,

Columbus lost his last friend at the Spanish court. King Ferdinand had no further interest in Columbus or any of his ideas.

For the last two years of his life, before his death on May 20, 1506, Columbus made repeated efforts to regain the governorship of the Spanish colonies. But he never succeeded, and he died a deeply disappointed man.

He had no way of knowing that the New World he had discovered possessed riches beyond anything the world had yet seen. And even more impossible to imagine was that he would be honored as one of the most courageous, far-sighted explorers of all time.